Christmas Memories

MELODY BOBER

8 Late Intermediate Piano Arrangements of the Season's Most Nostalgic Carols

The Christmas season brings a flood of wonderful memories from my childhood: trips to my grandparent's farm where the 15-foot tree was ablaze with light; the continuous buffet of homemade holiday treats; and the fellowship of aunts, uncles and cousins. These things truly made the holiday one of love and happiness.

Christmas morning was always exciting with the opening of gifts and discovering the treasures from Santa in our stockings. The day was complete with the reading of the Christmas story from Luke, Chapter 2 and the singing of traditional Christmas carols.

In *Christmas Memories, Book 3,* I share arrangements of some of my favorite carols. It is my hope that you enjoy practicing and performing the arrangements in this collection and that they will stir your hearts and re-kindle your own precious memories of this blessed season.

Merry Christmas!

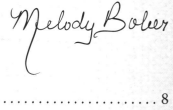

ALFRED

Copyright © MMVII by Alfred Music
All Rights Reserved

ISBN10: 0-7390-4916-X
ISBN13: 978-0-7390-4916-7

Joy to the World

George F. Handel
Arr. by Melody Bober

What Child Is This?

Traditional English Melody
Arr. by Melody Bober

5

God Rest Ye Merry, Gentlemen

Traditional English Carol
Arr. by Melody Bober

Away in a Manger

Traditional
Arr. by Melody Bober

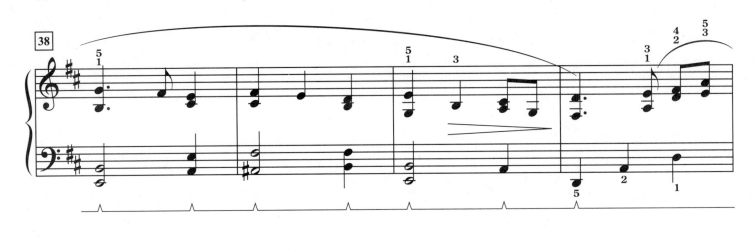

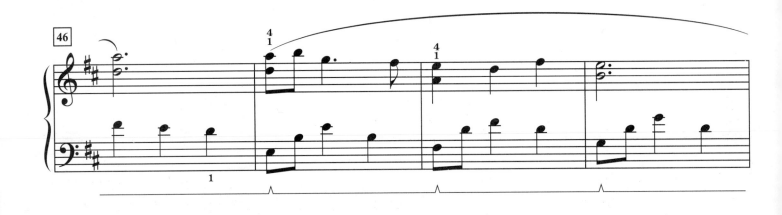

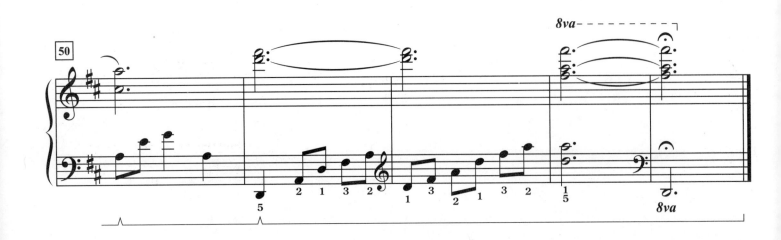

Jingle Bells

James Pierpont
Arr. by Melody Bober

* A swing tempo can be used, if desired (♩ = 108–112).

O Little Town of Bethlehem

Lewis H. Redner
Arr. by Melody Bober

The Holly and the Ivy/O Christmas Tree Medley

Old English Carol/Traditional
Arr. by Melody Bober

Hark! The Herald Angels Sing

Felix Mendelssohn
Arr. by Melody Bober